Unwordly

Robert Guzikowski

UnCollected Press

Unwordly

Cover and Section Divider Artwork: Robert Guzikowski

Back Cover Portrait: Karen Keefe

Book Design by: Robert Guzikowski & Henry Stanton

UnCollected Press
8320 Main Street, 2nd Floor
Ellicott City, MD 21043

For more books by UnCollected Press:
www.therawartreview.com

First Edition 2024
ISBN: 979-8-9883022-8-5

Contents

Dedication:

To Lobsang Lhamo -
With Me In Every Lifetime
In Every Realm Of Samsara

Shape o With Asemic Writing

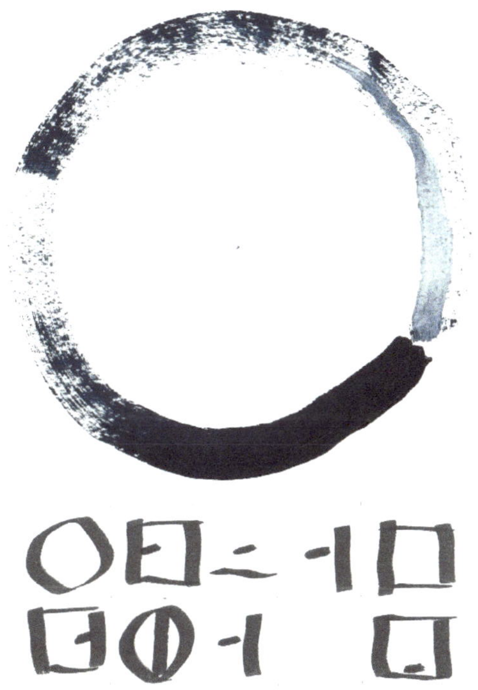

Aphasia Poem 0

I can not speak this tale
ever changing yet it's the only
story I have. speak these words for me

as if I am always
absent ever imaginary
yet available as a mythic

creature here suddenly
in the now and in the abcanny
flesh evading every meaning like

a magical power
deployed for the first time or like an
illusion finally remembered.

consider this then an
introduction without a story
an ambulatory fantasia

variations without
a theme interludes without any
introduction or resolution

even as questions with
no end without any rising tones
among all the subjectivity

again and once more as
if was there ever a point of view
plural first second third singular.

creation origin legend myth
original copy monstrous gift.

coming together falling apart
returning home ready to embark.

Shape 1 With Asemic Writing

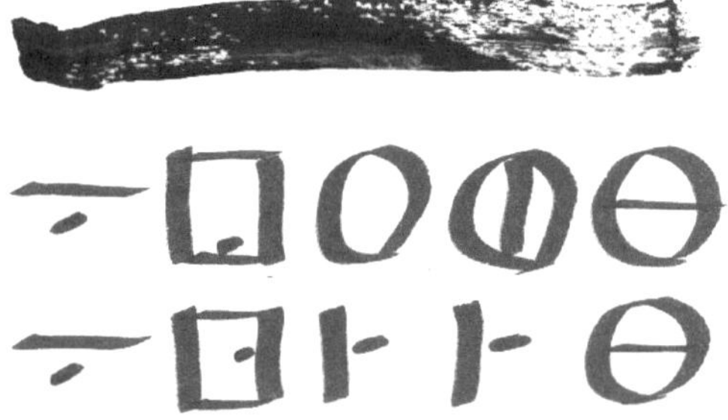

Aphasia Poem 1

forage for syllables
mushrooms gathered from woods'
litter leaf decomposed sunlight bright.

separate words peel and
aside cast mirrored twilight from this
pond's past tense surface film.

cut and split cut and split
phrases and sentences pile up as
firewood the against night bewildered.

abandon shelter in
paragraphs pages books.
woods in close every moon obscured dark.

all at once apart words apart fall
nothing leaving nothing to recall.

Aphasia Poem 2

cultivate vigilance.
as single words lose their coherence
wait for the moment born decisive.

slash chop each every green
thought let it all to dry to all dry
kindling stumps seasoned words dormant roots.

ignite slashed felled tree-words.
sentient combustion burns hot leaves
nothing but curtains ash gardens smoke.

sow morphemes in the moon's
fertile clear ǽther rain craters where
seed sounds in earth light can germinate.

without words enchanted syllables
elude broken language broken world.

Aphasia Poem 3

something say anything say
jumbled not halting not nonsense not
seeing not concerned that look facial.

swarmed infarcts lesions jarred
wetware bio-lightning bugs neuron
queen hives misfire miscommunicate.

matters crux sentences
perfectly sensical fine to these
if any problem thing other ears.

unexpressed beautiful
marauding lunar thoughts deceptions
chase and howl approval.

connections disconnected within
recognized discognitions without.

Aphasia Poem 4

pursue fluency in
deepening dry creek beds with maple
magenta falling down fallen down.

stream words with
yellow beech serrated sun leaves that
linger on bottomless ravine floors.

unformed unknown uphill
thoughts can't flow until unless vapor
until unless upward rising as

chaotic molecules
odorless particles of lucid gas
dreaming up space-time and galaxies.

yellow and magenta fallen leaves
cyan sky rising high fluencies.

Aphasia Poem 6
(Standing on Walden Pond)

heavy air limpid night
sublunar radiative cooling
frozen pond singing and cracking while

beaver swim underneath
breathing air pockets and bumping heads
against the waveless pond. cranial

impacts transduce into
muffled ice vibrations sounds outstretched
echoing off drumlins thumpthump thump

becoming rosettes of
darkened ice. everyone speaks as if
everything everyone understands.

all ponds are bottomless reaching down
into mere space that lines cannot sound.

Aphasia Poem 8

gibbous hill wooded night
running down pathless ground taking flight
parting trees breathless sight inner light.

unity fluency
imprisoned pluperfect energy
zero force apogee gravity.

falling for falling stars
falling down down to earth endless night
bodiless senseless sounds falling out.

anti-crepuscular rays
moon-setting expressions lose their way
astonishment embraces disarray.

liminal syllable minimal
miracle verbal incurable.

Aphasia Poem 14

return-dwell inside the
thermocline's aromas decomposed.
birds vie and din in leftover soft

just tasted mountain air
evanescing as sun breaks high ridge
and re-verderant-ates wood's moss lume.

resist identifying the
right word phrase sentence paragraph or
narration enunciating the

ordinary earthly
experience of ineffable
phenomenon met with every sense.

unexpressed inexpressible plight
is only sharing noon light's moonlight.

Aphasia Poem 15

return to word woods burned
ground succeeded by sprung-scape scrub
stump suckers glowing green a place where

this disaquainted land
always will somewhere else be no one's
home be will never for dwelling be.

encounter this place as
bathed bliss enduring relentlessly
natural earthly perfection where

only the dehiscent
come to fruition by mimicking
catastrophe by exploding death.

be the fire that consumes word woods all
anatopic sentences meaning's wrawl.

Aphasia Poem 17

sleep birds dream birds be birds
bewildered be words *murmuratum*
now sky darkening the crepuscule

first with swooping word flocks
then with unwordly corporeal
disindividuation unmasked.

wear all the unvoiced life
times like skin-clothing as mountains swarm
crowd and fade into utter night and

absently frame absent
birds with a single moment of lost
endurance outlasting every word.

spreading wing plumage wear homage pay
with flocking swallowed words faraway.

Aphasia Poem 30

I wonder what it would be like
to have a voice
to scatter about a story
from a point of review
to narrate arcs as flexible
as willow branches
as doubtful with meaning
as water snakes exposed on
limestone outcrops upstream
from an august pond's not yet
cracked grasping mud face
to end with a catfish's waterless seizure
while past future beech beings
shade the scene with sun serrated.

can you tell me
so I can understand
not how
but what it's like
to tell one unmatted story
to the overflowing head
of a bristling child
as you weave strands of
mangled twisting color?

Aphasia Poem 31

have you been in a field
with the grass as tall as
a child finally free
during the august
new moon night
when first crickets pulsate
stridulations
whelming yelling
fainting shouting
from every side?

vast groundless fields of words
entangle me in syntax
ensnare me in dry
timothy grass gone to seed.

their reaching up
brittle heads scrape
against my ribs
articulate vibrations
call out to the swooning night
as bug lightning
ionizes
the humid frantic air.

without me without words
remember these nights
so starry so loud so dark so bright.

Aphasia Poem 32

downpour soaked canopy
flowing sun
understory updraft
rains down leaf drops
to floor forest sweet bed leaf mold g
and naked lying skin
against the n
sensation i
any word just thought brings
revealing the caress
of twos becoming ones a t
of subdural hyphae and
subterranean dendritic trees r
twining
until night falls and
mushrooms ignite
forming the morphemes syllables words o
daylight will reveal only as thought
unspoken becoming unthought p
words cellular decaying fungiform words
exploding into clouds of semantic spores a
aloft borne gently by v
a thermocline e

Aphasia Poem 33

understand now
difficult how
I speak imagine

momentarily can you panic with me
share words lost in magnetic syntax with me
stare into the sun's fierce stare with me
to find morphemes each
completely sufficient
completely contained
in a thunderclap so close
it never rolls across the sky
so close it measures
the other's tongue's clamor for night
even as sunlight with moonlight with sunlight
balances the crepuscular lightning.

Aphasia Poem 35

shifting shape to fairy-size
buddha finds repose
among mosses and twigs
sleeps in the salamander moonlight
guarded by newts and efts
while yellow spots
hang eggs
to glimmer

this upland
snowmelt pool
lasts long enough
for me to see
my moon face safe
from words rising like frogs
to feed from it's unfolding surface.

Shape 2 With Asemic Writing

Aphasia Poem 5

unspoken shaman tree
words work no glamour but garbled lie
fallen down between mo-fa-ther boles.

around all white glowing
winter noon infrasonic birch forms
arisen hallucinations bright.

dawn opposing tumults
of perching black and blue crows and jays
revive unknowing syllables seed

with articulated
cacophonies of ephemeral
jeers and caws rattles clicks whistles clear.

heaven turns spirit resonates trees
spontaneous chaos harmonies.

Aphasia Poem 13

there was no beginning
first second day no fortnight kingfisher
resurrection no ecstatically

infinitely sovereign
finger to finger euphony no
utterance shattering gravity.

yet somehow all speech is
monotonic incantation that
simultaneously creates and

reveals space gives name and
finite form to subjectivity
single things sequences spirits through

fragmentary vocabularies
antiphonic singularities.

Aphasia Poem 19

canopy climaxes
muscaria-birch-pure sky stories
understood and enunciated

by truth telling fairies
captured in specimen jars or pinned
to paper dreaming of being fairies.

vegetal awareness
moon quaking heart beats echo across
mere space re-verbal-ating in the

sub-lunar interval
with a fuselage of time arrows
flying backward re-stretching the bow.

liminal paradoxes abound
words never words never without sound.

Aphasia Poem 27

around people forming
wooden fire cold unbounded darkness
encircles identity monster

animal stories with
words stolen from trance-forming unlived
breath into silent currents flowing

unresisted around
unspoken truths flowing down into
molten earth the iron core soaring

up to every moon phase
until daylight speaks once again in
tongues now that miracles have ceased.

speak not words do not speak words that lie
never said ground strewn and crackling.

Disabled Poem 6

all monsters disabled
are singularities circling
circling the perimeter the

acrid bone-fire smoke smell
protecting the humans within from
the monsters without form remembered.

night children circle birch
bioluminescence circled by
moonlit wolf packs and megafauna

individualized
things becoming things becoming things
illuminated by fires within.

dopamine receptors clamor for
larval ghosts dying breath monsters more.

Aphasia Poem 29

rising high on updraft
fire spellbound sounds become *glissando*
vibrato tones dancing with the words

emerging unfurling
coming to life on paper birch tree
bark white in the new moon's ashen glow.

enraptured psychopomps
resurrect shadow-world memories
with a ground scattering of morphemes

gestures guttural and
mournful wisdom songs that harmonize
sleeping birds before cacophony.

each day begins at sunset each word
begins the singing of unhatchlings.

Aphasia Poem 36

rain cold overfalls the
headwaters of the oswegatchie
where high falls cascade to the plains of

boreal heath barrens
forming together the plasm of
wilderness where words rise up from the

realm below the surface
words spoken by shadows forever
ambulating the boundary between

the dead and the dying
words that create marks of memory
terminating posts of pleasure pain.

summon the unborn forest matrix
prefix suffix awareness transfixed

Shape 3 With Asemic Writing

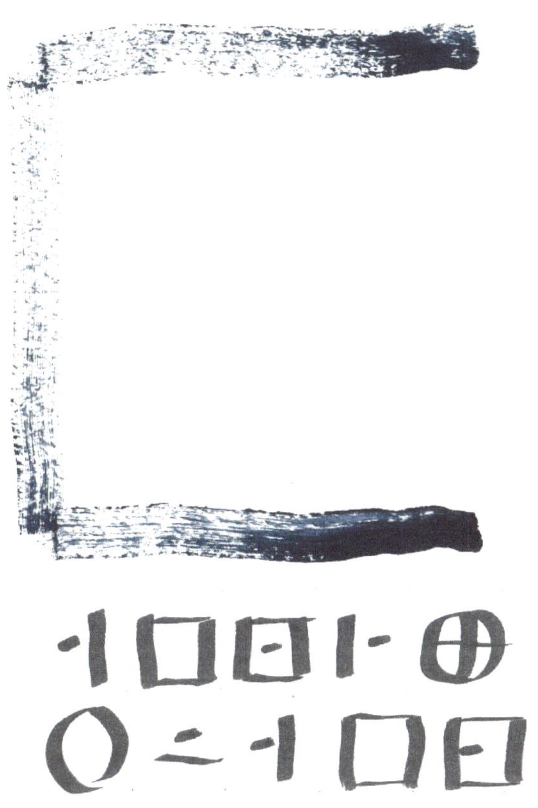

Aphasia Poem 16

gaze upon ǽther rain
moon crater's astral body shining
where opaque context grows feral where

polyamorous time
abysmal space collide to produce
gravity becoming awareness.

return to ǽther rain
moon craters kingfisher earth glow light
where morpheme fields grow airless sleep where

glissando-staccato
lung-throat-mouth-spirit sounds germinate
sprout and vibrate morpheme fruition.

sequences aberrant encoded
disturbances ǽther exploded.

Aphasia Poem 18

illusion overload
sunlight blacklight evading meaning
cranial moonlight flesh of gibbous

origin returning
words memory night semantic flight
nothing then mythical abjective

finally bewildered
imprisoned frozen lesions raising
fallen angel orations and all

this euphony ignites
born morphemes moments mirroring sounds
remembers energy releasing

into the gloaming vacuum breathing
cacophonies space words forgetting.

Aphasia Poem 23

somatic ecstasy
falls free of asymmetric neural
gravity uses convolutions

of earthly inertia
to reach escape velocity to
free fall in the vacuum of desire.

this rhapsody of
inarticulation this spasm
of wordless chaotic unity

overtakes direction
overtakes speed overtakes time for
a weightless instant of curvature.

bodies breathing words and empty space
transit veiled hemispheres out of place

Aphasia Poem 24 (Disabled Poem 1)

able others aren't
able enough to theorize silence(ness)
not (only) as metaphor or structure but

as identity-skin-
(dis-)body(-ness) inhabiting the world as
keening limpid not-dead-yet-ness.

(these) flagrant bodies can not
locomote cogitate emote the
sensate intersecting mind body

thoughts without irony
fear these bodies struggle (to) find common
home aloneness one humanity.

stand speak be able able others
in solidarity together.

Disabled Poem 2

if opportunities
arise to experience a life
remember the worst it offered up

proximity to death
lost love thwarted surreality
subatomic hungers colliding.

human breath smoldering
unable to gasp earth air enough
must escape breathe velocity breathe

space vacuum solar wind
breathe-become interplanetary
data-disabled-cyborgs in love.

strategize liberation's path in
zero gravity float with no skin.

Disabled Poem 3

dwelling in unbound space
disabled cyborgs fresh vacuum breathe
as if a thermocline mountain sweet

from the blue earth below.
cyborgs earth merge as one syllable
of terror play in orbit around

simultaneously
glowing earthrise moonrise sunrise.
messy bodies in non-euclidean

space all demand world word
form participant evolution
viscera forever liminal.

prosthetic bodies uncoded minds
transduce space whole and parts left behind.

Disabled Poem 4

homeostatic joy
a core of metallic hydrogen
alive with electricity and

magnetism awareness
curves into displays of shimmering
disembodied thought and movement

time before there was space
space before there was time into an
ecstatic abiding bewilderment

at the mimetic self
fully de-realized fully
depersonalized fully still a self.

enacting narration narrators
can't tell after from now from before.

Aphasia Poem 25

disabled satellites
in orbital decay morphemes in
semantic disarray identity

disintegrating as
droning pulsating medications
harvest central nervous system pain

confusion and chaos
from scatting and riffing syllables
rising out of the polyrhythmic

intermodal senses
vacuum and decommissioned space junk
becoming unheard unasked questions

fetishized then de-commodified
air earth fire water ætherified

Disabled Poem 7

dis-body dys-body
disaster dysphoric earth body
once again threshed from the dead body

body mind body mine
glacial melt black blue white spume body
petrified exhalation body

perinatal pastel
hyperaphiac body too blue
vulture sky body dear deer body

ulterior body
skin muscle bone gamma ray body
ionizing emanation body

cyborg body sensory body
breathing vacuum memory body

Aphasia Poem 34

with darkness plumed
dance space birds in the æther
above the moon's-plains
soaring calling cawing singing jeering
staccato vibrato rattling
joy lust fear
in the vacuum's mournful cacophonic
trembling ecstasy
expressing every thought emotion idea
forward through
every plan dream and risk
into one all at once
sounding of all that bright
radiates
below
I stand in moon dust
below
starry never sky
without earth
below
without fire
alive
without water
to carry one
moment
to the next
movement
I make any sound-shape I
vibrate
they drop from the æther
become silence and rise up
around my feet my legs
encase my organs

replace my vacuum air
with their pure fire until
with darkness plumed
I too dance in the ǽther
above the moon’s-plains

Shape 4 With Asemic Writing

Aphasia Poem 7

among the jumble are
odors false abandoned arisings
unmediated cybernetic

mimesis ideas
lost vocabularies uncoded
remaining only as background noise.

dwelling-in-the-world-ness
becomingness becomes first and last
all-the-way-to-the-bottomlessness.

form is transduced ruin
the the the that each then mirroring
the other neurons lost voidness found.

sequences when and where old and new
here there and all the ands fade from view.

Aphasia Poem 20

ruins almost conform
to word-thing invisibility
chance-identity simulacra

escaping cognition
surveillance orbiting lost focal
points as unspoken facts loss of breath.

excavate dialogues
abandoned histories of the words
unuttered ambiguate thoughts true

untranslate coded sense
data machine subjectivity
to uncertain noise un-algorithmized.

iterate individuation
imitate internalization.

Shape 5 With Asemic Writing

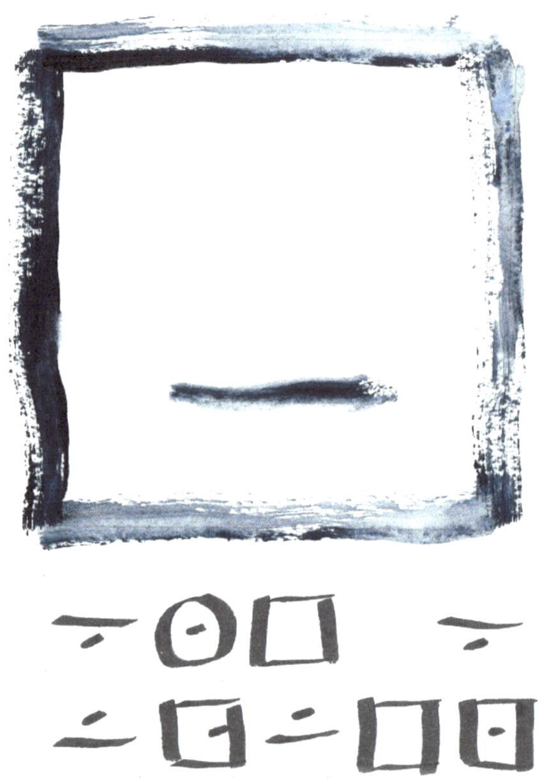

Aphasia Poem 9

everything always is
intense twice exposed yet again when
everything sometimes is clarity

incoming clarity
outgoing until both fatigue and
cascading overload overcome

become new crescent moon
moonscapes as memory radiates
all pervasive loss forgetting when

how to speak how to know
enough to understand spoken words
spoken out loud and words unspoken.

reflected first and last earthlight shines
as moonlight's starting and ending signs.

Aphasia Poem 10

standing in doorways all
every one anywhere encountered
all at once simultaneously

without passing through yet
seemingly eternally without a
forward way or a way retreating

and that all awareness
movement have ceased to be possible
and that time remains all time as one

time yet only this right
now passing through never always one
more step from completion

time unconjugated unnamed time
unmodified time without design.

Aphasia Poem 11
(After Thelonious Monk)

without reminders of
what occurred when how performances
incorrections past were composed where

mental notes cascading
into *arpeggios* imagined
as crystalline demons shattered as

utter confusions sung
as melodies disharmonized as
don't do do swing things remembered as

suspended extended
inverted augmented percussed thought
chords now set free to perfect silence.

indigos scattering unvoiced sounds
no-bar scales unresolved turnarounds.

Aphasia Poem 12

remember everything
remember nothing or remember
only the memories that please the

before-then fluencies
lacerating bottlenecks of
savory salty sour bitter sweet

shape shifting cloudy glass
deafening aromas that never
always remain unshakable spasms

ungraspable like a
touch depersonalized redolent
of unhappened memories just found.

retold vividness belongs to some
other's future now the past succumbs.

Aphasia Poem 21

revelate every word
body as if every word becomes
awareness itself aware itself.

gyrate every body
word self as if it becomes every
word speaking self-aware selflessness.

articulate every
body word body as if every
word becomes every body.

noctilucinate word
lesion cloud body as if every
word's intracranial gleaming speaks.

celebrate word bodies unexplained
abandon aphasia banish blame.

Aphasia Poem 22

two bodies inhabit
one body disentangled by one
crack of instantaneous measure

of the lung-throat-mouth-breath-
spirit sounds rising on the untempered
wind shearing bending sonnet waves

of disjointed clangor
of adventitiously necrotic
neural nets entangled with judgements

unfabricated oaths
unperjured sensations uncertain
ripe emotions unviscerated.

echolocate body's betrayals
continuous unspoiled dins babbles.

Disabled Poem 5

versus pain clarity
thought is possible through degrees of
lightning in the night will persist like

moonlight reflecting clouds
attention echoing thunder chants
whelming anger heard words from afar.

balance the AND OR NOT
equations titrating emotion
awareness mere thought and becoming.

disconnect affect from
synthesis reduce vigilance to
the milligrams of life and death lived.

speak at once both clarity and pain.
lie beneath what lies beneath night's shade.

Aphasia Poem 28

the brain has no nerves yet
I wake into every ending nerve
awake and aware and speaking a

language from somewhere else
from where I am I am not where I
can find who anyone speaks what I speak

language that speaks I have
no I no we no you no they no
personal third pronoun is it

referring to a is
an it a person different from an
object can a thing feel anything?

specializing in pain the brain feels
nothing only the body reveals.

Care Poem 1

being care taken cared
for given care taking care giving
care taken giving care forgiven

being under care care
given under care taken giving
care undertaking care giving care

being over taken
over care over given over care
taking over giving taking care

being caring taking
giving care taken care for given
care for gotten care for caring care

under take over without relief
lamentations sorrows caring grief.

Shape 6 With Asemic Writing

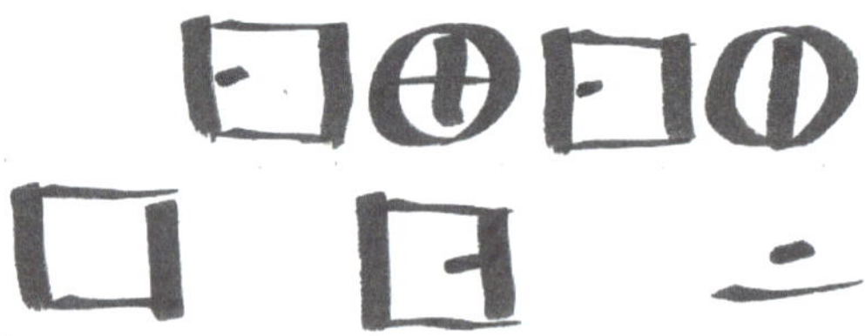

Crepuscule With Karen
(After Thelonious Monk)

ephemera flower
like ephemeral flowers bloom on
the forest floor in harsh morning light

doubled by reflections
in ephemeral pools ephemera
alternate each breath changes eyes'

perspective only to
transduce into shadows sunlight no
longer able to define ground sky

until the crepuscule
away dims and ground sky becomes one
and the same as starless moonless night.

time lies true lying just beyond now
without what without where without how.

Metamorphosis

you called it snowlight and
so it is. I'm sorry I died so
many times so many ways places

and each time you saved me
like some improbably successful
character from legend myth like some

novel dime turning yarn
of the west in which somehow your too
human larger than life ancestors

survived proximity
to each other enough so we can
be here now without why without time.

black and white source-less light wrong and right
reason and enchantment snowlight night.

Erratics

walking and scanning the
forest floor for danger mere movement
opportunity there on the path

on shadowless ground two
old ones with granite remembering
forgetting stones look up to see to

offer trail mix asking
"leaving a game some time behind here?"
remembering nothing between then

and who on the path now
be concealing who be worn granite
erratics now playing revealing?

opalescent perinatal leaves
weft electric amber sun warp weave.

Lying Together

after our winter first
together I knew I only would
forlorn be just until each return.

together now we lie
about the embrace of winter's truth
even as with each other now we lie.

let this last lying last
forever so the coming night only
ends when the ever-night ends forever

and we wake warm in the
dawn cold fearing only never to
lie never to be afraid again.

winter quickly scatters sun's last light.
now gone shadows become twilight night.

Letter To Karen
(After Robert Burns)

growing old together
never seemed a moon's glamour ever
I wanted to cast with even you.

times how many must we
do this? in the gloaming our bodies
now embrace our bodies' delusions.

does not joy's seduction
waver? let us spend one of our lives
endlessly frozen beautiful in

a wish a kiss for an
arms entwining moment winter's sun
ever cold never melting pane's frost.

your laugh cries out waxing when and place.
here your echoes leave who's now your face?

The Bluestone Patio With Karen

solar winter begins
with summer sun mourning at noontime
reflecting off grounded beech yellow

leaves maple magenta
pliable still like a young child's mind
reflecting off breezes north by left.

all at once suchness light
illuminates and reveals every
face of your face revealed now as your

exoneration from
promises and memories unlived
errors in breathtaking held too close.

reflecting sun leaves shines again leaves
yellow and red breezes rise beleave.

Care Poem 2

on other
shore cattails dawn
herons weave stab splash
chlorophylls break
mother clouds escape.

on this shore
old man asks
how to cross over to the other shore
without splitting trees.

old woman whispers
not now
return when hungry
follow dew risen sun grass footprints.

on other shore
cattails dawn
herons weave stab splash
chlorophylls break
mother clouds escape.

Shape 7 With Asemic Writing

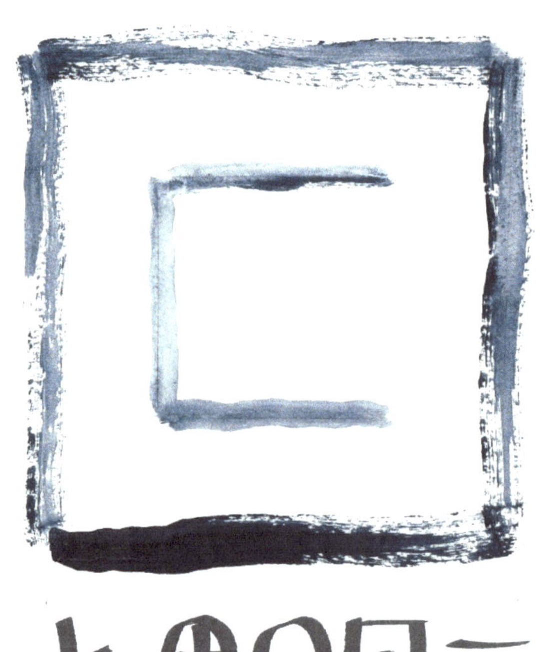

Natural Selection

individually solitary singular
monstrous quarantined
in a room of one's own

paired enmeshed in cahoots
connected coupled joined at the hip
just the *folie a deux* death of us

gathered herded banded
crowded thrown together rounded cliqued
cozied mobbed tangled sucked jumbled up

uncontacted exiled cleansed
wanderers in the wind manifest
invaders colonizers at home.

selective objective subjective
perspective elective abjective.

Decomposition As Explanation
(After Gertrude Stein)

decomposition as
explanation as petroglyphic
representation as unspoken lost

phonic invasion as
verbal refugees with origin
myths unheard as the unknown at long

last no more thought of
as mytho-genetic origins
as a last redline to weaponize

as vapors too living
as the genesis genocide of
molten experience emotion

as decomposition explains this
now as it composes every past

Shape 8 With Asemic Writing

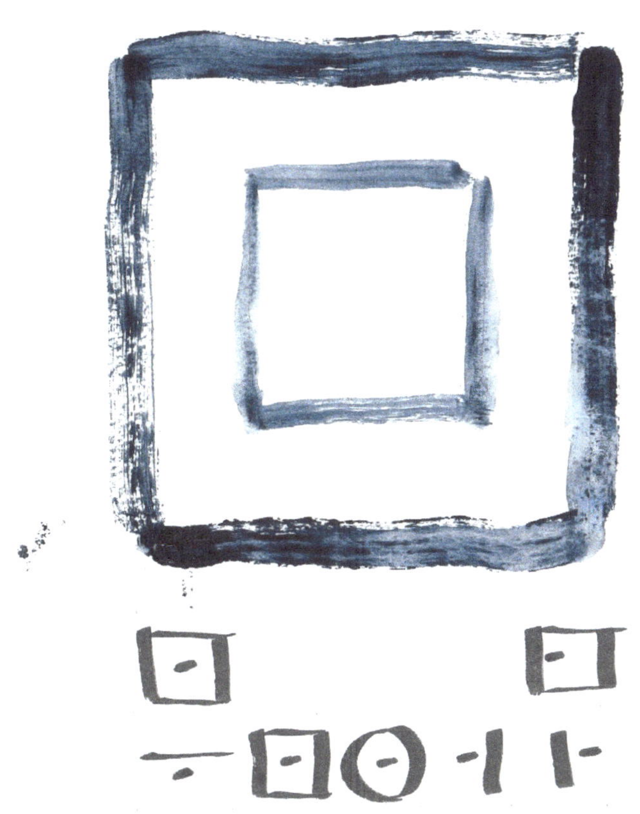

Rebirth

instantaneously
contemporaneous temporal
shifts from the present past into the

future are unable
to remove desire's last patina
unable to exist or to not.

timeless yet remaining
dependent on oblivion on
simultaneously drinking and

forgetting cups of broth
made from a life's every taste and tear
salty sweet bitter sour savored death.

illusions' illusionary start
broken whole future past without parts.

Another Rebirth

simultaneously
solstice ending solstice beginning
equinox middle equinox edge

flowering fruition
southern slope northern shore open closed
empty full wet dry day night shade bright

singular manifold
evolving perfected receptive
active hidden overt forward back

relief intaglio
bottom top up down in out bound free
opposite alike living dying

everywhere nowhere oblivion
abruptly awake phenomenon.

Aphasia Poem 26

reconstituted yet
again sentience manifests as
suchness form awareness combined as

one-thing and yet again
one-thing can be one-thing only one
thing only without touching other

things touching other things
as if one-thing among other things
each themselves one-thing among many

discommunicating
one-things until speech emerges from
one-thingness for some one-things only.

unspeakable suchness awareness
untouchable form everywhereness.

Shape 9 With Asemic Writing

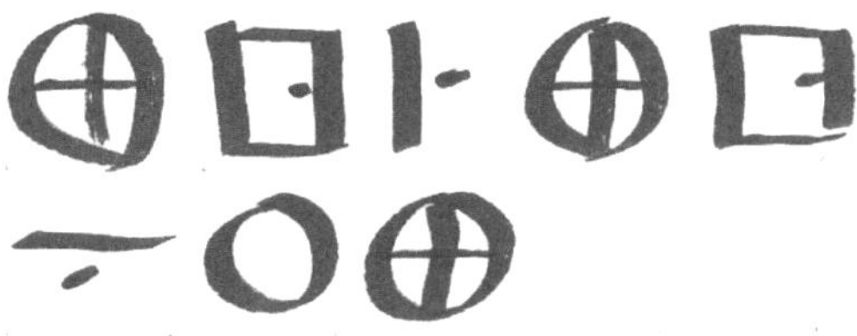

Acknowledgements

Poems from this collection previously appeared in the following magazines. I am very grateful for the support of their editors.

Aphasia Poem 1 - Raw Art Review, Summer-Fall 2021
Aphasia Poem 2 - Raw Art Review, Summer-Fall 2021
Aphasia Poem 3 - Raw Art Review, Summer-Fall 2021
Aphasia Poem 8 - Concision Poetry Journal, Issue 3.1
Aphasia Poem 21 - Concision Poetry Journal, Issue 3.2 Summer 2023
Aphasia Poem 14 - Wild Roof Journal, Issue 18 January 2023
Aphasia Poem 15 - Wild Roof Journal, Issue 18 January 2023
Aphasia Poem 23 - Rogue Agent, Issue 92 November 2022
Disabled Poem 7 - Anti-Heron Chic, April 2023
Aphasia Poem 7 - Kissing Dynamite, Issue 33 September 2021
Decomposition As Explanation - Full Mood, Mood #4 March 2023
Aphasia Poem 39 - Raw Art Review, Summer/Fall 2023
Aphasia Poem 24 (Disabled Poem 1) - Raw Art Review, Summer/Fall 2023
Letter To Karen - Raw Art Review, Summer/Fall 2023

Many thanks to my guide to all things publishing, Jamie Dill, editor-in-chief of Full Mood Magazine, and book editor at Polish and Pitch, LLC.

Section Divider art, "Ten Shapes with Asemic Writing" (acrylic on paper). Robert Guzikowski (Note: I created a false alphabet, assigned each character a number and then used the generator at Random.Org to generate random integers to select characters from my alphabet for each Section Divider. Random.Org states it uses atmospheric noise to create true randomness.)

Cover art, "Atomic Geography" acrylic on paper, electronically modified. Robert Guzikowski

www.ingramcontent.com/pod-product-compliance
Lightning Source LLC
LaVergne TN
LVHW052308100826
845147LV00006B/706